CW01213672

Journey Through BACA

Poetic Characterisations

GORDON GRIFFITH

authorHOUSE

AuthorHouse™ UK
1663 Liberty Drive
Bloomington, IN 47403 USA
www.authorhouse.co.uk
Phone: UK TFN: 0800 0148641 (Toll Free inside the UK)
UK Local: (02) 0369 56322 (+44 20 3695 6322 from outside the UK)

© 2022 Gordon Griffith. All rights reserved.

No part of this book may be reproduced, stored in a retrieval system, or transmitted by any means without the written permission of the author.

Published by AuthorHouse 07/29/2022

ISBN: 978-1-7283-7421-5 (sc)
ISBN: 978-1-7283-7420-8 (e)

Print information available on the last page.

Any people depicted in stock imagery provided by Getty Images are models, and such images are being used for illustrative purposes only. Certain stock imagery © Getty Images.

This book is printed on acid-free paper.

Because of the dynamic nature of the Internet, any web addresses or links contained in this book may have changed since publication and may no longer be valid. The views expressed in this work are solely those of the author and do not necessarily reflect the views of the publisher, and the publisher hereby disclaims any responsibility for them.

Scripture quotations are taken from The Living Bible copyright © 1971. Used by permission of Tyndale House Publishers, Inc., Carol Stream, Illinois 60188. All rights reserved.

Acknowledgements

I want to say a special thank you to the following individuals who have impacted my creative writing and development as a poet:

Anthony Roberts, my primary school English teacher from St Christopher Primary School, Barbados

Robert Maurice, my English Literature teacher from Boys Foundation School, Barbados

Anthony Hinkson and writers of the Barbados Creative Writers Workshop, who introduced me to writing poetry

Sis Belle, New Testament Church of God, Barbados who suggested I enter the Barbados National Independence Festival of Creative Arts (NIFCA) where I won my first national gold award for poetic characterisation

Anthony Copper who taught me to edit my own writing, Trent University

Dr Jack Wolfe who provided a critical analysis of one of my poems, Masters Creative Writing, Open University

Dr John Lunnun, who graciously read these poem and wrote a foreword which referenced names I had not heard before and sent me to YouTube to do further research

The late Sis Livingstone, New Testament Church of God, Nottingham who promoted my gift and after my poetic performances called for encore, to raise funds for the Church.

Finally, I want to thank God for the gift of poetry and my family who supported me throughout the writing, rewriting and performance of these poems.

Foreword

A journey through the valley of tears: Psalm 84.6 'as they pass through the valley of tears they make it a place of springs, the autumn rains also cover it with pools'.

Songs are often likened to poetic composition with music, with this compilation it can be said that poetry has found its blues voice.

These poems articulate the anguish and the denial over history of the cultural contribution and acceptance denied to people who are regarded as marginalised and outside the spectrum of ruling elites and the establishment.

They follow the struggle to be heard; from the visceral scream for freedom of the enslaved in 'Voyage' to the arbitrariness and injustice of colonisation; 'Granny Creole'. They address not only physical but the emotional inheritance of the children of the enslaved and colonised and how it is carried deep in their subconscious.

From Rap to calypso in 'Other Brother, 'Blessing' and 'Nottingham' these poems pay homage to early calypso songs such as Lord Kitchener's 'London is the place for me'[1951] and have a similar rap beat. Whilst 'Three Badd Boys' offers a grime sensibility. In 'St Ann's Well' the poet offers up an ode to place and the ancient gods of water such as the Celtic goddess Coventina.

This poetic journey contemplates the difficult choices growing up presents us with; loyalty to family and societies norms or to break free and create a new start in another place. Yet as the poet shows 'I saw him die' and in 'Time' how often these are circular journeys as we often return to the once despised family fold and home. 'Time' carries a melancholy beat much like its namesake from Pink Floyds 'Dark Side of the Moon' [album 1973].

These poems riff on biblical texts and parables offering meaning outside of scripture and theology. In 'Blessing' a rethink of Psalm 23 [king James version] is reminiscent of the Srawbs song Lay Down [Bursting at the Seams album 1973] and holds a musical rhythm resonant of a congregation at prayer.

'Dear Mother', 'Old Joe's Christmas,' 'Do it Right', 'Oasis of Love', 'The Real Deal', 'Marriage' and 'Disco Fever' explore sexual awakening and different forms of love with an openness and joy of the body whilst Disco Fever highlighting the beats and flashing strobe lights celebrates the raw passion of sex. These poems following in the tradition of Ovid and John Donne also open new experiences as Bernadine Evaristo has done in her lyrical novel 'Mr Loverman' [pub2013]. These experiences often ignored by mainstream society, they address how love/sex impact on individuals and their families.

I'm pleased to recommend this collection as a welcome addition to the many diverse cultural voices now being heard and recognised within Britain's cultural scene bringing as they do an often regrettably forgotten or deliberately ignored part of Britain's cultural constituency and heritage to light.

John Lunnun, BA(Hons), MA, PhD.

Introduction

Journey Through Baca is an anthology of poems that epitomises my life. It reveals some of my darkest moments and celebrates my resilience through creative humour and poetic characterisations. It begins with 'Genesis', where the voice of God thunders through the ages within a drumbeat, captures my hopes, dreams and disappointments in 'Metamorphosis' and culminates in my hope of being raptured.

It brings me from the Garden of Eden in the heart of Africa, to the home of my grandmother in Barbados and from the Caribbean to Nottingham, the world's best city, according to some.

I rebelled against everything I knew and tried to carve my own way in life. After many unsound decisions I returned home having learnt my lessons and made my decision to turn around my life.

These poetic rhymes, characterisations and inspirations document my journey to hell and back. They expose my emotional distance travelled as expressed in the poem 'Dear Mother' where an empowered man writes to confront his mother about the emotional abuse and neglect, she put him through.

These poems are my personal journey, but they resonate with the universal journeys we all take in this life, to varying Degrees where raw emotions, pent up feelings, disappointments and ecstatic elations come to light. Every poem is a life changing moment and as you read them you will identify with the voice and the emotions of the speaker.

Genesis

Out of the still black night
The tear-filled eyes
The dust
And fragments of time

Out of the drumbeat
The heat of frustration
The catapult
Of perpetual stillness

Out of the naked rib
The pain of regret
The anger
And broken cords of life

Out of the crushed dreams
The long-forgotten hopes
The survivor's cry
Poetry is born.

Voyage

Africa was raped
and I was ripped
like an aborted babe
from her black belly.

I was licked
with stick
with whip
on a ship
was sick
was kicked.

Over wave as a slave
I came,
in chain
in pain
inflamed with anger.

Naked, cold,
sold as cattle
as chattel.
In the marketplace
disgraced,
not a trace of my race,
could scarcely stand
as a man.

I worked land
on plantation,
with hoe, with Joe.
Long before cockcrow
I go,
in rain
in cane
insane.

I ran from hound
underground
was found
was bound,
was beaten
was broken
was bruised.

I refused to suckle
to knuckle
to buckle.
I wept.
I crept
pass slavery,
lost identity
searched for ancestry.

I found emancipation,
tiptoed through colonisation.
It was a desperate situation.
I crawled fast
I crawled pass

white pages
of Black history.

Another ship,
another trip,
all the while
I struggle
to be free.

Granny Creole

Granny rises with the first speck of light
in the Eastern skies, and starts her day
with a long, long prayer
for she grandchildren.
Before the cock crows Granny gets up
and makes a cup of Milo
to break the air from her stomach
before she goes.
Some people say Granny is slow
on her feet; but Granny is sleek
and she moves with the beat
of the times.

Every day Granny wobbles her way
to the bus stop;
under the load of light bill, water bill
now she has the extra weight
of a telephone bill.
Still, every day that God sends
Granny bends her way to the bus stop.
She fears the school rush and squeeze
so Granny eases through the early morning breeze
alone,
as clerks, teachers, nurses pass
without the friendship of a smile,
Granny waits a while, hugging her flask
close to her bosom.

Every day I can still hear Granny's voice,
'Now look here children, and listen tuh me,
I gon tell whunnah something,
Be good and do what whunnah should;
Go to school and learn well,
But remember,
If whunnah doan guard whunnah soul
Whunnah gwine straight tuh hell'
Granny would say.
Granny's task is her grandchildren,
untilled soil rich with fertility
and every day
she wades on to the bus-stop,
breadcrumbs in her basket.

Granny stands at the bus-stop
hands akimbo, back bent
beneath the weight of her ancestry,
slavery's scars cutting deep
into her soul,
eyes, burnt with age, strain
as they drag the lazy bus
around the corner
by the old dried out standpipe,
where she brought
many bucket loads of water
as a little girl.

Now Granny sits in the bus
one hand on her basket,
miles of memories drift behind her.
Granny's face is full of wrinkles,
not worries,
aging strings of thought
and she sings 'Amazing Grace.'
Granny trusts in hopes
long turned to God,
as she waits
in the marketplace.

Her tray plays a sad tune of survival.
She spins her sing-song rhythm
of price and goods;
she watches until the sun
melts, turns to blood
and falls from the Western skies
and dies,
like she too, one day will die.
Granny watches all these things
before she returns home
to the house that Jack built.

I Saw Him Die

At age fourteen, I saw my grandfather die
I stood around gazing, I wondered if I should cry
I felt ever so guilty, but I couldn't tell you why.

My parents were in England and I was on my own
I often visited grandpa at Uncle Hammard's home,
My father insisted I went to see him,
So little to see, his shrunken frame had grown very thin.

I remember Grandpa lived in Silver Hill
I felt forced to go and see him against my fourteen-year-old will
I had no one to talk to, to share my deepest thought,
Every evening after school, I walked, and walked, and walked.

First, they took off a foot from ankle to the toe
Then the doctor said, 'Everything below the knee must go.'
Then they did the same, with his other shrunken leg
'Please stop cutting him,' I really wanted to beg.

Both legs were gone now, cut off to the hip
For the first time I knew why they called grandpa, Nabit
A village name meaning diminutive in size
How fitting for grandpa, I now realised.

I wanted him to die and when he did
I didn't know if I should cry.
I locked up my emotions and put them on a shelf
While the family mourned, I simply blamed myself.

I didn't cry, I didn't lie, I didn't say a thing,
I could not feel the sorrow his death was meant to bring.
I watched it all from a distance, feeling very unsure
Because I had never experienced death like this before.

The Prodigal Boy

Bible study and prayer every day
I couldn't take it anymore, I had to get away.
Daddy said, 'It's a house of love and joy.'
I guess I was born to be a wayward boy.

I gathered my things and packed them in a bag
I had to leave that house; it was too much of a drag
And with all my possessions in hand
I took my journey to a faraway land.

To some far-off city, I said I'll go,
What I'll do there well I just don't know
But I have lots of money and possessions too
What gives me pleasure, that I'll do.

I started with marijuana, I turned to crack
But with all those drugs I didn't stop at that
And every day I was living for a high
But down inside, I felt ever so dry.

You see, my father's teaching was not for me
I had to make a name in this far city
With wining and dining and women like mad
I couldn't help myself, I spent all I had.

Then, with money and possessions all gone
I lost my friends because I couldn't carry on
With wining and dining, and living in sin

While in my soul there was a great famine.

I had no one to lend me a hand
And very soon I was a desperate man,
I joined the poor who slept on the street
And many days I had nothing to eat.

Suddenly, I remembered how it used to be
In my father's home before this far city
Even the servants had something to eat and drink
But look at me, man I started to think.

I will arise and go back home
It's better than staying here and having to roam.
I know I'm not worthy to be called his son
After all these wicked things that I have done.

With tears in my eyes and pain in my heart
To my father's house I made a brand-new start
And when he saw me, he ran with his arms outstretched
He never once said, 'You miserable wretch.'

Instead, he hugged me, he kissed me, he fell on my neck
He got me the finest clothes and a thorough welfare check
He put a ring on my finger, brand new shoes on my feet
He spread a table with every kind of meat.

He put on some music and led the dancing too
He called his friends and neighbours, man I'm telling you
My father is my one true friend,
And this prodigal boy will never leave home again.

The Other Brother

Imagine that!
You can imagine that
all these years I sweat for this man
got wet for this man
worked my fingers to the bone
never left home for this man.
Yet, after so long,
he never played a song for me
never talked about me, his son
loyal and strong,
all he ever does is work my soul-case
to the ground.

Day and night, I work
I never leave to go anywhere,
now I come home from the field
tired, hardly able to walk,
can't raise my hand,
can't lift a fork to my mouth,
and all I can hear
is the sound of music, loud and clear,
roast beef and fresh bread fill the air,
I stop someone and ask,
'What's happening in there?'

Tell me the truth,
do you think this is fair?

I never went with a woman
gamble or swear.
I work in the field with sickle and hoe;
many days I almost
chop off my big toe.
I chase thieves
and wild dogs from the flock.
I step on broken glass
and cut my foot on the rock.
I didn't have time for women or wine
I build up my father's bankbook,
I never steal a dime.

Now this worthless, no-good
brother of mine, comes back home
after spending all his money,
he doesn't have a penny to his name,
all he ever does, is bring my father shame.
Right from the start he broke
my father's heart.
He never lifted a hand to help the old man.
Look at my finger, all bloody and tied with string
while my brother has the diamond ring,
the finest gem in the family
and the very best clothes
for my brother, not me!
Now my father calls all the neighbours
to have a party and has no clue
why I am not happy!

When my brother left home
with all his possessions in hand;
my father changed, he became another man
he wouldn't eat or drink,
he couldn't sleep at night,
he would sit and watch until the morning light!
And I was the one, who put him to bed,
I was the one, who shaved his bald head.
Now this son he thought was dead,
has come back to life my father said!
So he calls all his friends, and neighbours too!
Not to show them what his hard-working son could do;
but to say his son that was lost, is found,
the one that was blind, can see!
Yet my father cannot see why I am not happy!
Tell me something, you think I should be?

Well I'm not!
I may be out of order, but I do not ask for a lot!
Just for a little acknowledgement
of what I have done,
that I stayed at home, never had any fun.
I work twice as hard
to do my brother's share!
And now that he has come back
like some superstar,
do you think I really care?
I think it's time I too run away
because to tell the truth
I cannot stay around here.

I am going to leave tonight
while they have their chat
but unlike my brother,
I'm not coming back.

The Good Samaritan

I was living in Jerusalem
Everyday just trusting Him
Then I started reasoning
'Life down here isn't easy
I hear that in Jericho
Now, that's the place to be
For there was lots of opportunity.
I made up my mind
I'll go down there and see.

Granny tried to talk me out of it
Saying, 'There is too much risk in it'
But I said, 'It's worth the risk
Cause I don't want to spend the rest of
My life in a place like this.'
It's not like I'm dissing it
It's just for me, this ain' it
I want sometimes to be kicking it.

I ran out of the city
Down through the valley
Passed one mountain then two
I heard a voice behind me say, "Hey you."
I turned to look back,
I heard a loud smack
I thought my skull was cracked
Someone struck me with a baseball bat.

One man punched me in the stomach
Another stabbed me in the back
Two more jumped out from behind a rock
One said, "Hand over everything you got."
But I couldn't move a muscle
I was paralysed with fear,
Granny tried to warn me
But I just wouldn't hear.

I reached for my wallet
I heard my neck snap
I thought I was dead
Cause everything went black.
They took all my money
They took all my clothes
And if that wasn't enough
They just poured on the blows.
I can't remember what happened after that
It was the guy with the baseball bat
But when I catch myself
I was naked, laid out on the track.
I heard a little noise and open one eye to see,
I knew I was safe because it was the pastor
But all my hopes soon shatter
When I realised he started walking faster.

As I lay there bleeding to death
I started thinking to myself
There isn't any mercy left.
I closed my eyes and started to pray.

I thought God had answered
When I heard some footsteps coming my way.
It was the deacon, but he only came to peep
Because he ran off as soon as I tried to speak.

These are God's servants and they didn't stop
My hope was fading, every last drop,
Then I heard a donkey bray
I thought, 'Thank God, He answered my prayer'
When I looked to see
I knew I was dead for sure this time
Because the man on the donkey
Was an enemy of mine.

I braced for the kick
And waited for the spit
But through my haze I was amazed
I could see in his eyes
There was mercy.
He cleaned up my wounds
Poured on His oil and wine
But I couldn't help thinking
This man is an enemy of mine.

He put me on his donkey,
But he was my enemy
He took me to the doctor.
I'm telling you, this man treated me proper
He never left me alone

He cared for me as if I was one of his own
Then he took me to a recovery home.

He asked for the owner
And gave her some money,
But this man who was my enemy
He told her to take good care of me
And don't let me lack, if it cost more
He'll pay her the rest when he passes back.

It was all a puzzle, a mystery to me
A pastor, a deacon and a sworn enemy
But of these three, he was the only one
That stopped and had mercy me.

Pray Fuh Me

Pray fuh me Pasta
Pray fuh me,
Pray fuh me Bruddha
Pray fuh me,
Pray fuh me Sista
Pray fuh me.

Each and every day
Just fall on yuh knees and say me ah prayer
Pray fuh me Pasta
Pray fuh me,
Pray fuh me Bruddha
Pray fuh me,
Pray fuh me Sista
Pray fuh me.

Some days I wake up and I feel so strong
Get outtah bed
Den tings go wrong,
Sometimes I feel so weak
Can't stand on muh feet
I look through de cupboard
Not ah thing to eat,
At times I go along
My face wear ah smile
But muh heart wears ah frown
Cause all life's problems

Just getting me down

Pray fuh me Pasta
Pray fuh me,
Pray fuh me Bruddha
Pray fuh me,
Pray fuh me Sista
Pray fuh me.

Each and every day
Just fall on yuh knees and say me ah prayer
Pray fuh me Pasta
Pray fuh me,
Pray fuh me Bruddha
Pray fuh me,
Pray fuh me Sista
Pray fuh me.

Sometimes I watch life pass me by
I sit down here, and I start tuh cry
Cause all muh bills and all muh pills
Like two mountains that keep rising
They pile so high and I pray to God
That I would die,
But if you think there's hope
Before I pull this rope

Pray fuh me Pasta
Pray fuh me,
Pray fuh me Bruddha

Pray fuh me,
Pray fuh me Sista
Pray fuh me.

Each and every day
Just fall on yuh knees and say me ah prayer
Pray fuh me Pasta
Pray fuh me,
Pray fuh me Bruddha
Pray fuh me,
Pray fuh me Sista
Pray fuh me.

When you fall on your knees
I'm begging you please
Call out muh name, again and again
Say Lord come by and heal his pain
Touch his body, soul, and spirit too
Show him sumting he could do fuh You
Gie he one spark o' hope, just to see he through.

Pray fuh me Pasta
Pray fuh me,
Pray fuh me Bruddha
Pray fuh me,
Pray fuh me Sista
Pray fuh me.

Each and every day
Just fall on yuh knees and say me ah prayer
Pray fuh me Pasta
Pray fuh me,
Pray fuh me Bruddha
Pray fuh me,
Pray fuh me Sista
Pray fuh me.

Reflections

I watched him
hop about
and bob
his head
from side
to side

I watched him
skip from
branch
to branch,
tree to tree,
so innocent
so free

I watched him
clutch
his claws
and cock
his head
and roll
his eyes around.

No care
no fear
no home
to call
his own.

I watched him
go
from day
to day,
from night
to night,
no fuss
no fight,

if danger
comes his way
he simply
takes his flight.

I watched him
fall
to the ground
and die
and thought…

Metamorphosis

When I spread my wings in splendour
And rise in the early sun-soaked skies,
To mount my nectar sweet
Pollen-filled morning glory,
Do not envy me.

Do not be fooled by my cool rise
Like a ghost from my host plant,
For I came this way through pain
And a process I found insane.

They said I would change from what I was
To something else, but no one told me what
So I watched the clock
And plot my path through life.

I wanted to be a dog and water the plants
With one hind leg raised and my spurting hose
Spouting a clear cream liquid on the grass,
But one day that liquid fell on me.

I wanted to be a cow with bulging breasts
And surplus milk for calves and humans too,
But one day I saw them take the cow away
And she has not returned until this day.

I thought I'd be a lamb to dance and frolic
Without fear,

But then I heard the lambs loud cry as a sea eagle
Found its prey.

I stopped wanting.
I decided to wait for my time of change to come.
Some days I cried and felt depressed
And tried to hasten time along.

It's no fun being a caterpillar, especially in this place
All the little children come around and pull an ugly face.
I ate the leaves my mummy said were very good for me
And if I only wait my turn, it'll turn out well, I'll see.

I waited and waited and waited still
Till my friends all disappeared,
And all I had to keep me sane
Were those strange creatures fluttering in the air.
I never quite did get the name,
Of those lovely silent things
I called to them, but they never heard
They had such beautiful wings.

Slowly, my body shortened
I too began to change,
I knew I'd never be some creature grand
I was a disappointed man.

I must have slept for ages, at least a week or two
But when I next emerge into the light
I spread my wings
and took my flight.

Blessings

I am no rapper
no Ice T or MC Hammer,
no Bad Boy turned Good
in answer to Rhianna.
Sometimes I miss a beat
sometimes I start to stammer,
but God gave me something to say
and I'm going to say it in a way
that even hip hop can understand me.

When the devil comes knocking
to show me what the sinner man is rocking
and I have nothing!
I long for those things,
then I think about Jesus
and I drop on my knees.

The more the devil comes
stressing me,
depressing me,
the more I want less-o'-me
and more of Christ in me,
until my soul can clearly see
and my testimony can only be
that the Hand of God is blessing me.

I have a roof over my head
clean sheets on my bed,
food on my table
a shirt on my back
shoes on my feet
I'm on Instagram and WhatsApp.
The Lord is my Shepherd
and I am His sheep,
when the wolf pounce upon me,
before I can bleat
the Lord jumps in the way
whilst I lay down in peace and sleep.

This valley is only a shadow of death
and I'm walking through,
the Lord God is my help
and my comfort too.
When the storms come against me
All I have to do, is stand still
And pray, Lord I'm trusting You.

Although I don't have the money
to buy a brand-new Nikkei
or give my wife genuine Gucci;
even though I'm an outcast from my family
I've learnt the Lord God is my Jehovah Nisi.

And it doesn't matter me
how the devil tries to batter me,
I know he cannot splatter me
because Jehovah comes a-back-o' me
this is not the end-o'-me,
I triumph o'er my enemy
Jesus comes and sets me free
and every day
I walk in faith and victory.

Just Ah Little Boy Called David

I'm Just a little boy called David
Just ah little boy called David
Just ah little boy called David
Just ah little boy called David.

Eva day I gwine out dey
Watching father's sheep.
Up come ah lion and tekkup one
Sey he gwine down dey tuh eat
Man I got so mad, I ran so fast
I grabbed dat lion
And kill he in de grass.

Den up come dis bear (roooaaaar)
Tuh fill my heart wid fear
And tekkup ah lamb
Like he doan care,
But wid de help o' God
I went down dere
I took my lamb
And I slew dat bear.

And
I'm just a little boy called David
Just ah little boy called David
Just ah little boy called David
Just ah little boy called David.

Now I does get so vex tuh hear
Goliath out dere like he doan care
And God's mighty army… living in fear.
Eva day I could hear he say
'Send me a man tuh fight me out here,
I would kill him dead
And feed him tuh de beast
And dat's the way dis war will cease.'

Well I can't tekkit nuh mo'e
Tuh hear he say
He will kill any man we sen' out dey
So I went to duh king
Whose name was Saul
He gi'e me his weapons,
His armour and all,
But I can't wear dem,
I too small.

I'm just ah little boy called David
Just ah little boy called David
Just ah little boy called David
Just ah little boy called David.

So I tek off Saul ting
And I tekkup my sling
Cause I gwine out dey
Tuh do God's ting.
But when Goliath see me
He started tuh laugh

He hold he belly and ben' up in half,
He thought I was a little joke
He thought I came tuh mek mock sport
He asked me if I tink he is ah dog.
It is den I tell he
Bout de lion and de bear
I said, 'Goliath, my God is here
If you knew dat
Your heart would be fill wid fear.'
But Goliath just laughed as he came near.

So I twirled my stone
And hit he in he head.
De next ting I know
He dropped down dead,
And I tekkup he sword
And cut off he head
Just tuh let he know
Our God dread.

And
I'm Just a little boy called David
Just ah little boy called David
Just ah little boy called David
Just ah little boy called David.

Now listen tuh me,
My little friend,
If God did it once
He'll do it aghen.

So don't le' dem mek you
Backup in fear
Don't le' dem mek you
Pull out yuh hair
Wid God in yuh hand
Yuh gottuh be strong
Bring dem giants
Down tuh de ground
Kill dem dead
And cut off dhum head
And let dem know
Our God dread.

And
I'm Just a little boy called David
Just ah little boy called David
Just ah little boy called David
But I'm ah mighty man of God.

Three Badd Boys

Ben' bow or burn boy
Ben' bow or burn.
Ben' bow or burn boy
Ben' bow or burn.

Now Ne-bu-chad-nez-zar
As the story is told
Was a king of old
Wid an image o' gold
And all through the land
He had it say
Dat when de music play
Yuh got tuh bow tuhday.

So when yuh hear
De music sound out loud,
Yuh gottah bend down low
Wid de rest o' de crowd.
Doan stan' up straight
As if you proud,
Cause de fire in de furnace
Crackling loud.

Ben' bow or burn boy
Ben' bow or burn.
Ben' bow or burn boy
Ben' bow or burn.

Now eva man jack
Duh gaddah down dey
In de market square.
De music start
Duh bow down low
Cause duh heart now fill wid fear.

From de North and de South
From de East and de West,
De music start
And boy its de best!

De rich and de poor
De weak and de strong,
When de music start
Duh haffah bow down,
De Black and de White
De Yellow and de Brown,
When de music start
Duh touch de ground.

Dem bend down
Bow down
Crouch down low,
Cause eva body know
De king say so.

So when yuh hear
De music sound out loud,
Yuh gottah bend down low

Wid de rest o' de crowd.
Doan stan' up straight
As if you proud,
Cause de fire in de furnace
Crackling loud.

Ben' bow or burn boy
Ben' bow or burn.
Ben' bow or burn boy
Ben' bow or burn.

But three badd boys
Like dem cayne hear,
When de music start
Dem turn deaf ear,
Dem stan' up straight
Like dem doan care
And eva body now, looking in fear.

When de king look round
He start to frown
Cause he saw dem boys
Dat wouldn't bow down.
De king get vex
And start tuh flex,
'Go fetch dem boys!'
And fuh miles around,
Yuh couldn't hear ah noise.

So when yuh hear
De music sound out loud,
Yuh gottah bend down low
Wid de rest o' de crowd.
Doan stan' up straight
As if you proud,
Cause de fire in de furnace
Crackling loud.

So ben' bow or burn boy
Ben' bow or burn.
So ben' bow or burn boy
Ben' bow or burn.

Now when dey got tuh de king
He was not please
Dat dese badd boys
Dint bend duh knees
When eva since he had it said,
If ah man din bow
Tuhday he's dead.

But de three badd boys
Just calmly said,
'Dis god aint real,
Dis god is dead.
But we serve ah God
Who's alive and well,
And de fire in yuh furnace
Aint nuh match fuh hell.'

'We'll see bout dat!'
De king reply,
'And in dat furnace
Tuhday you'll die!
I gonna heat dis furnace
Hot as hell,
I gonna let de fire
In dis furnace swell,
Den I gonna pelt you in
One, two, three,
Who is your God?
Tuhday we'll see!'

So when yuh hear
De music sound out loud,
Yuh gottah bend down low
Wid de rest o' de crowd.
Doan stan' up straight
As if you proud,
Cause de fire in de furnace
Crackling loud.

So ben' bow or burn boy
Ben' bow or burn.
So ben' bow or burn boy
Ben' bow or burn.

Now de furnace was heated
More and more,
And all around was heat galore.

Den de music sound
But dey diddunt bow down.

So de king command,
'Go pelt dem in,
Dese three badd boys
Dat would not sin!'
And even duh men
Dat pelt them in
Like de king had said
Couldn't stan' de heat
Duh drop-down dead.

But de king just watch
In great delight,
Cause dis was his time
Tuh set things right.
Den sudden so,
He face start tuh turn
Cause de three badd boys
Just did not burn.

'We pelt in three!'
De king den shout,
'But look, dhum is four,
Quick, tek dem out!
And let dem go
Cause I neva see
Such ah ting befo'e!

And now
Let de whole earth know
Dat dere is no odduh God
Like de God
O' Shadrach, Meshach and Abednego.'

Nottingham

Nottingham, is de place tuh be
From Top Valley,
Leen Valley
Or down dere in Strelley
Evabody ought tuh be
A part o' de strategy
Tuh mek Nottingham
De world's best city,
Whether Trent FM
Or Trent University.

Immense diversity
Economic sustainability
Regeneration
Developing de community
Health and education
Better situation
Even for de people in Clifton
Lenton
Living long in Wollaton.

We mekking life a betta quality
Fuh everybody,
Dis is de Nottingham strategy.
Through renewal
Social inclusion

Betta housing situation
And leisurely recreation.

More open space,
Development teking place
More houses and allotments,
Not a piece of land tuh waste
And when we get we money
Out of Iceland
We could bring you sea, sand and sun
Right here in market square,
In Nottingham.

We reduce de flooding,
De knife and gun crime
And tuh mek de city cleaner
Our bin men are at your doorstep
Eva week, regular and on time.
We keep Nottingham city moving
And we bring yuh betta transport
Whether it is bus, tram, train
Or canal boat.
So lend a helping hand
And mek our city bloom
And when we switch off duh lights at night
Guh fuh ah walk, enjoy de moon.

From Bulwell to Clifton
Bestwood to Wollaton,
Through Basford, Berridge
Hyson Green and Arboretum,
Radford and Lenton

Sherwood, Mapperly
Or St Anns,
Castle, Dales or Meadows
Leen Valley and Bilborough

A plethora of activity
Even if like people in Top Valley
Or my friend in Strelley,
With or without
TESCO Extra in yuh community,
Whatever yuh situation
Dere is sumting fuh you
Right here In Nottingham.

My St Anns

I first met you at church.
Strange that,
I didn't think of you
like that.
Actually, I didn't think
of you at all
until one day I got the call,
Black on Black violence
is about,
the word is out,
if you're from the Meadows
St Ann's not a place
you want to go,
and although I knew
I never thought of you,
then I found you on the Internet,
the opportunity to meet you
was perfect.
Others said I might live to regret
yet, I knew that all
the stories I heard
could not be true.

I learnt that I would work with you,
I felt unsure
I did not know what I wanted to do,
hold you, embrace you

touch you, smell you?
It was crazy, I didn't know you
Still, the rumours started;
you are bad for me,
not my type of company.
I made my stand,
reached out, took your hand,
felt the hard, rough skin
your gritty voice,
the unkempt nature that
ran wild in your veins,
I had no choice.

I looked at you,
dull eyes, thin frame
I didn't even know your name.
Overgrown jumpers
and baggy tracksuits bottoms
hid your frame
left you overlooked in the drain
of a culture that corrupts,
until time touched you,
gently wriggled its way beneath your blouse
pumped life into your jumper
filled it with laughter that leapt up towards your eyes,
your face flashed a smile in response,
boosted the contours of your tracksuit
and smoothed your sharp edges.
I saw you smile,
I saw you dressed like a flower

Erupted overnight,
Fragranced, in full bloom
Petals spread like raspberry ripple
Adding flavour to looks
And silence to rumours.

Although I did not tame you
restrain you,
could not boast that I changed you
rearranged you,
I grew fond of your
dark, mysterious past.
I learnt your liturgies,
ate your food,
looked past your faults
and the rumours I heard.
Now I'm part of your
future, included in your plans
and at last,
at long, long last
I can truly say,
'You are my St Anns'.

Images at St Anns' well

Healing waters
Robin Hood's barters
King James Easters
Night trips dip
Beneath moonless skies
Cries of street lovers,
Tradition.

Farmers planted, waited
For liquid life
To flood the valley.
Meeting point for grandma,
Aunt May
Distant cousin Sally
Charlie
And uncle Frank,
Who stank of stale beer.

The well spits in the pints
Of a council
Who refuses to bend,
To secure her heritage,
Her night life
As her story lives on
In the tales of the town.

Lips met
Mingled taste of wine,
Fragrances merged
Drowned in forbidden seas
Of love sought
Love brought to king size
Duvet.

Life At The Centre

The Centre sat smack at the top of the hill,
Hunger Hill in St Anns
Where it is said, King Henry the second rode through
And stopped at the acclaimed well, for a spell
And passed through the now nationally recognised allotment.

Three buildings, each of a different size
None of which could win a prize for modernity, efficiency
But each has its own history, its own legacy.

The watchman house that sits by the gate,
Two bedrooms on the top floor,
A kitchen, dining room and shower where a small toilet
Stood tall and thin like Watchman Jim
Who would not let you in through the black gates
Without your membership pass.

The second building was an old school
Converted to a bar and social club,
Where members came and played dominoes and snooker,
Or like errant schoolboys,
Some hid in the back rooms to play poker.
An annex was added and converted to a health suite
Where others came for a back rub
To have their hair and nails plucked or polished
Or their body healed by reiki.

Across the car park was a newer building
Downstairs a computer suite for IT training,
A manager's room and open hall,
But upstairs three large classrooms and a huge kitchen
For Friday night shebang, with jerk pork and fried chicken.

These three buildings are often used for Luncheon Club,
Day Care and late-night parties
Or wedding receptions, funerals
And social or family activities
Which many considered a real fire hazard
With its hall that should only hold two hundred people
Being packed with a thousand.

I often imagine what it would be like
To meet the Bishop there one night
A beer in his hand, and a strange woman at his side
I heard he used to go there before I took it over.
I did see him once, but that's nothing to talk about
He was playing dominoes and he drank a guineas stout.

Weekdays

Long shadows loomed in my living room
Spicy candles glowed.
A cold breeze squeezed through the vent
I sipped hot coffee.

My silence exploded into scampering feet
Children up and down stairs
Shouting at each other through thin walls
Unaware of their neighbour.

I would leave earlier for work this morning
Give myself an extra half an hour
To meander among cars parked ad hoc to block pavements,
Forcing prams and pedestrians onto the road.

I would follow streams of blues and greys and greens,
Watch mothers juggle umbrellas and little hands and
Shout for excited feet to wait at the crossings
As seas of smiles giggle and jostle their way through the school gates.

Jason

He was hated by some, discriminated against
But he wouldn't stand still, an example to the saints
A pushy go-get-it character with a bit of a driver trait,
He didn't take corners, just kept it on the straight
He wouldn't wait for the green light, convinced he was right
He kept it tight, day and night in the fight against wrong
He stayed strong until the very end.

Project after project, from place to place
Jason was a young man
With no time to waste on silly tittle-tattle,
He was a soldier in the heat of a battle
No opposition could bind his vision
Matthew 28:20, was his great commission,
He held nothing back; he would die empty
For a newcomer at his age, he did plenty.

Taking piece of the city, bringing peace to the city
He was doing fine, a stalwart in society
Inspiration to community, negotiation with authority
He clothed the naked, fed the hungry
Threw out a lifeline, tackled knife and gun crime
He was a visionary doing the extra ordinary
He died young, but his life is legendary.

Stepping Out

Called like Paul
to preach, to teach,
each day I help
another soul lay hold
on the goal of eternal life.
Salvation through Christ,
who paid the price for sin
so that we may win this battle of life
through Him.

Some refuse to pay the price.
They chase the ice
and throw the dice,
while we sacrifice
to get to know Christ
and the power of His resurrection,
to share in the fellowship His suffering
all the while becoming more like Him
through strife to gain our inheritance
our crown of life.

By His death, He left a legacy
for those who are ready
to press ahead
and leave behind
the things that bind us
trick, trip and flip us,

the devil's lie.
But whether threatened or beaten
bound or imprisoned
we will not relent.

The time spent,
knees bent in prayer
fully aware that this
is not a hit-and-miss.
Our faith conquered kingdoms,
obtained the promise,
stopped the mouths of lions,
put out fires,
broke the enemies' sword
and put them to flight.

Sometimes we are stoned,
shipwrecked
mocked at
shot at
But we cannot stop at that.
If it is our lot to die for Him
we still win.
Our body was sold to sin
like grain to gin
but after that, we'll rise again.

Call us ignorant, fools, insane
we boast,
not because we think we know the most,

or that we can take out an evil host,
because we are filled with the Holy Ghost.
We know we are weak
so day and night we seek
the face of Him whose grace still amazes us,
who called us out of darkness
into His marvellous light.

We fight the good fight of faith,
we have victory
over every plan of the enemy,
so we remain on the front line
all the time,
preaching and teaching,
reaching souls for Christ.

Time

Time is always with me
Like love, I have to find it
Like money, I too often spend it
Like water, I try not to waste it
Like my favourite movie, I sit and watch it

Time is always with me
First thing in the morning
Last thing at night
In the dark and in the cold
When the swallows take their flight.

Time is always with me
Like the sunshine in Summer
The fallen leaves in Autumn
The chilled winds in Winter
And the blossoms that leap for joy in Spring.

I once climbed a mountain
I dived to the ocean's depth
I once rode on a dog sleigh
And flew on the supersonic jet.
In all my experiences
I held the hand of time,
And now that I am aging
I do not really mind.

Angry Reflections

The pesky little thing
ignored me.
He hopped about
and bobbed his head
from side to side
like a burglar on the prowl.

He skipped from branch to branch
and flicked from plumb to plumb
and pecked the ripest fruits,
then hid himself among the leaves
obscured from my view.

He clutched his claws
and scratched the flesh
and rolled his eyes around.
Each damaged plumb
a penny down
and every penny makes a pound.

Uncaring, fearless, he puffs his breast
and calls my tree his home,
I shooed him off
he squawked at me
and comes again to feast.

'It's just a bird,' my neighbour said.
But to me, he was a beast.

I Got Tuh Start Tuh Witness

I got tuh start tuh witness
And witness with a zeal,
I got tuh start tuh witness
And witness to succeed.

I got tuh start tuh witness
Everywhere I go
I got tuh start tuh witness
Cause duh Bible tells me so.

I gwun witness tuh de old
I gwun witness tuh de young
I gwun witness tuh de feeble
I gwun witness tuh de strong

I gwun witness tuh de Black
And witness tuh de White
I gwun witness tuh duh
Even if duh colour ain't right.

Yes I got tuh start tuh witness
And I starting from tuhday,
Wid muh big black Bible
I'm off on my way.

De first person I see walking down de street
Is a very ole man, nuh shoes pon he feet,
He trousers full o' patches and all covered wid dirt
And believe you me,
You could never guess de colour o' he shirt.
When he pass me, I go'ng pretend I ain't see
Cause dere is no way I go'ng witness
Tuh somebody looking like he.

Here comes a young woman in one short, tight-fitting skirt
I sure she just wants dis Christian man tuh flirt,
And see how she throws she hips all bout de place
Me, witness tuh she
I ain't got dat time tuh waste.

Here comes a white man in he three-piece suit
And ah brief case in he hand,
I go'ng le' he go long bout he business
And I go'ng stand right hey and witness.

Now here comes a rasta man
He hair all tie up like rope,
He got more beard on he face
Like he is some billy goat,
And he singing one o' dem rasta song
Dis time he now come from smoking dope,
Me, witness tuh he
You must be mekking joke.

Wait, de Lord like He don't want me tuh witness tuhday
Cause evah since I hey
And up tuh now He ain't send ah single soul my way,
You know what,
After dis short word o' prayer
I go'ng leave dis witnessing tuh some oddah day.

Dear Mother

I know you may not want to hear from me.
For years you said I was fat and ugly
but I want you to know Mother
that today I am happy.

I found out for myself how true love can be
I've met a man; his name is Trevor.
He doesn't mind that I'm not very clever,
when we are in bed and our flesh rub together
sparks fly and I experience an unnatural high.
Sometimes we try to hug and its pitiful some may say
because our bellies just get in the way.
So, to truly connect we take turns from behind
and I am telling you Mother, Trevor really blows my mind.

You may never see how this ugly fat slob
could be truly happy, but I am,
your words, deleted from my mind, like spam
as I walk hand in hand,
shoulder rubbing, fat wobbling
I'm smiling back at my man.

I don't lock myself away anymore
and cut my leg like I did before,
I don't let bullies taunt me
and say I am fat but cannot fight,

I don't sit in silence
as they slap my back to see my flesh jiggle.
Trevor has taught me to stand up for myself.
My face is always aglow,
if you could only see me now Mother
Just one look and you would know,
your son has found true love.

I didn't lose weight and build up those muscles
I'm still no He-man and may never be your hero
but one thing I know, I'll never be a total zero,
just a man who has found love in the arms of another.
Now our hearts are knitted together and with every touch
I shudder, with every thought I smile, I smile Mother,
I fall asleep with a smile on my pudgy face,
a warm hand on my muffin-tops waist
and a breath of love on the pillow next to mine.

So Mother, I hear you are divorced now,
dad left you for another,
your years in the gym,
neat waist, right diet, Botox lips,
stylish hips, implants,
didn't keep him at your side.
I hope you don't ever have to hide
the loose skin tuck-up under your chin
or the plastic covering over your grin.
I hope you never wake up alone in the night
Crying, looking at yourself in the mirror
because you have become ugly.

You see Mother I know what that is like
and not even you deserve that plight.

I am still your son,
if you find it in your heart to receive me,
believe me, I would come running
with Trevor at my side.
I know he would love you
just because I do.
He respects me, never neglects me
adores me, makes me feel loved.
He became my mother love and father care
and whenever he is near,
I know Christmas has come and
it's another year of happiness and bliss.
Mother, I never thought that I would ever live
to feel like this.

My dear, dear Mother,
if you could imagine one moment of happiness,
that's just the way I feel right now,
with Trevor kissing my shoulder as I write
whispering in my ear 'It's all right.'
Every time a tear-drop falls, he holds me tight
then releases me to carry on this fight.
If I don't hear from you, Mother,
I understand.
I still love you and I forgive you.

Well that's all from me for now,
a few months more and I'll be dead.
I can see that smirk on your face
But this is my honest to God answer
I'm not HIV positive, Mother
The doctor says I have cancer.

Ole Joe's Christmas

When I think about Christmas
I think about sex,
I said that to my Church
And the people got vex
One woman in the pew
Shout, 'Lord Jesus what's next.'

They called it sacrilege,
I call it privilege
Now pastor telling me
'Ole man
I think you need a pilgrimage.'

But I am a very old man
With a young woman at my side
All these years I waited
Just to make her my bride.
Now every night
This woman in my bed
You could imagine the thoughts
Going through this ole man's head.

But I can't touch my woman
'til this baby Jesus born,
So nine more months I wait
For my first Christmas morn.

I say, Away with the manger
Swaddling clothes and Baby too
I just want a chance
To do what married people do
Get my woman out Jerusalem
And sow a seed or two.

I hear how they said
This Baby isn't mine,
She too young for me
And I wasting my time,
But all I think about
Is Mary in my bed
And the first chance I get
To quench this fire in my head.

All these years of looking, longing
All these miles of walking, knocking
knowing everybody's mocking.
But now it's my turn
To lift my gift from its stocking.

At last we arrive home
And I have my chance
At making some children of my own
Cause all along, I couldn't do a thing
'til the shepherds heard those angels sing
But now, it's all up to me.

So, I don't care how you vex
When I think about Christmas
All I think about
Is sex.

Oasis Of Love

I see you naked, wet, exposed,
A rose, a gem,
Mayhem of pleasure, a treasure
I measure you with my eyes,
In my heart
The start of chaotic passions
Fashions my longings and
Carves you into my dreams
.

I reach out to hold your hand,
On the sand
We form patterns and watch
As the sea washes them away,
Silhouette against the sunset
I kiss your neck
Gently, like a butterfly
I call for you in the night

I hear you breathing deeply
Calling sweetly to me,
We touch, fires flare
Your lips hot against mine
Your breath flames on my face,
Your moist skin takes me in
And I am lost in your depths,
Cocooned in your embrace.

Love in a Felt Tip Pen

There is a fragrance in my head
As I sit beside my bed,
And it tells of the loveliness
Of you.

There is a feeling in my heart
Once together we'll never part
From love forged in fire, so strong
So true.

There is a pain in my mind
The loneliness I find,
While waiting in a world
So blue.

There is a tear in my eye
And a pen in my hand.
There is a thought of you
And a plan,
To bring us closer together
Forever.

My Wedding March

I saw you
walking down the corridors of time
and you filled my mind
with dreams.
I wanted to fill your life
with beautiful things.

I ran after you
I called to you, but you did not hear me
I kept on running
I kept on calling until you turned around
I looked into your moist brown eyes
I realised I had found love.

Now that I have found love
I never want to let it go,
I want us to flow together
down the streams of life,
I want to wake with you beside me
I want to sleep with you in my arms.

I want to touch your hair,
kiss your lips, feel your body next to mine.
I want to hold you,
squeeze you, fill my life with you.
And now that you are mine
I know I will never let you go,
unless you want me to.

The Real Deal

Our eyes locked,
my heart stopped
my blood cells collided
my tongue stuck to the roof of my mouth
my breath solidified like colourless bogey
frozen in my nostrils.

My mind worked overtime
calculating the still pulse,
willing my body to move, to function.
She stood poised and looked at me,
her hair fell like a waterfall
her shoulders succulent marshmallows.

Her face like candyfloss,
my fairy-tale queen,
the idol of my dream,
the beam that fell from the rainbow
and I the clumsy bear
that cannot stay afloat.

She walked towards me,
I watched me watched her as she came closer
leaned forward, her breath like strawberry ice
she asked what my name was.
I tried to answer but my lips did not move,
she leaned forward and kissed my cheek.

Electric shock, waves,
sparks flew,
saliva drained from my mouth.
My heart started again,
the dream was over and my queen
stood shaking me awake.

Fighting Back

I have earned the right to cry
to scream,
to erupt in violent response!

I am not a violent man,
but I can
meet violence with violence,
laughter with smiles
and sorrows with tears.

I am a man.

Not a big man,
not a bad man,
but a man.

Cut me and I bleed,
oppress me for too long
and I respond
like a man.

My actions are not right
but neither are they wrong,
for sixteen years is too long
to suffer in silence,
smile when I want to frown.

Judge me now and find
I am a man
of the humankind.

Let me laugh with you,
cry with you,
pray for you.
But abuse me
and I will have nothing to do with you.

Deliverance

The police came
and I went with them.
All I took
was a Book and a prayer.
I couldn't think
of what else to do
so Lord Jesus
I held on to You.

The mountains shook,
the lava flowed,
destiny and man
met in the shadow.
They looked each other in the eye
and destiny bowed,
the man didn't die.

Lilac walls,
sultry rooms,
coffee cups,
no mops
or broom.
Computer drones
night and day.
Another cheap room
And I'm on my way.

Sunday became Monday,
Tuesday became weekend
then Sunday came again.
I'm a man in waiting
I no longer live for laughter
nor feel the pain of anger.

Revival

He wants to rekindle
the fires, the passions
lost within her hollow
blue eyes,
to see them widen
like sun-soaked skies
after the rain.

Her matted hair,
a snare falling down
her shoulders
like serpents spewing
their venomous hiss
kissing her neck,
heckling her.

She smells of garage oil,
abandoned car fumes
and stale sweat.
Her deep-well dimples
curve like half moons
and her heaving chest,
once the red robin crest,
now deflated.

Like cumulonimbus clouds
that spill their guts

and bleach their usefulness
to the earth
and masturbate over the sea.
He looks at her weight loss,
loose bones wrapped in loose flesh
In tight jeans.

Her frail hands no longer caress,
crush zits, unzip his trousers.
Her ankles, adorned
with bracelets, with beauty
smooth to his touch, tattooed,
not cut and scratched.
Shapeless, meaningless, thin.

He stalks her, she falls for him,
punches his chin like a boxer
lightweight as a feather,
She flies into his arms as he falls
from the surprise.
Too late she sees the mischief
In his eyes as he kisses her

Simple, cherry-based lip balm,
the palm of her hands against his chest
as he presses his lips against hers.
Who cares that they had not spoken?
Their lips parted to exchange passion
not words,
meaning teeming through his veins,
dreaming only of the hollow in her eyes.

She smiles, he sighs.
Instant lovers, like three in one
coffee pack
waiting for their blood to boil,
for the perfect brew
true to the last heated breath.

Maybe it was the crack cocaine
cruising through her veins,
marijuana clouding
her brains,
the loss of two children,
the fever,
her zero-size model diet,
anorexia
her childhood abuse,
being nude on youtube,
selling her body on ebay,
the gaunt look on FaceBook.
Maybe it was his inability
to provide for her.

He watches her and
a gut wrenching cry
calls from somewhere inside of him,
his lips do not move,
only his eyes tell the sad story
of his love.

Disco Fever

The mad dash
The wild rush
The kaleidoscope of colours

All out feelings
Riding high
On naked nerves

Soft strokes
Stepping up
Breaking down

Melting into the push and pull
Of volcanic pulse
Exploding into rhythmic tones;

Eyes locked in blinkless flutter
Feet slip and slide, hop and spin
Hips rip and rise like clothes
In the wind of percussion drums

Bounce around on a thin line
Skin lined with charcoal
Beaded with sweat
Until wet.

My Wife

She is my wife
The love of my life
The one I keep safe
And free from strife.

She is my sister
Who never fails me,
The one I honour
And vow to protect.

She is my gift
From heaven above
The one I cherish,
The one I love.

She is my story
The only one I write,
She's my glory
Who fills my heart at night.

She is the one
With whom I share
My body, my blessing.
She is my inspiration
She is my friend.

Woman in My Head

Last night as I slept upon my bed
I saw the most beautiful woman in my head.
I woke up quick
To find, she had already given me the slip.

I tried to sleep to keep her close
But she had already gone I supposed.
Then I fell asleep again
And for a while I tossed and turned.

She didn't come, she wouldn't show
I held my breath so I wouldn't snore.
It didn't matter, I'd missed my chance
Now I'd never find that true romance.

I awoke a disappointed man
My wife woke me up, my coffee in her hand.
And very soon I realised the woman in my head
Was standing there beside my bed.

Marriage

The cold moon flared in the dark sky
Melting my brow
As I wiped dew drops from my face
From my wasted life
That rose out of thin air
Thin ice, twice as elusive
Twice the dream I never shared
The feat I never dared to pursue.

I watch blue skies turn black
Turn back dark clouds
Bringing birds and bees and green leaves
To sleeping trees
Awaken by butterflies
Fluttering wings
The sting of death, the breath of life
Filtering through the sunlight.
I see you, perfect in my mind's eye
Contrasted against my life's lie.

Do It Right

Don't hesitate
Check to see if you satisfy your mate,
Don't keep trying to fake
Sex is not some seductive bate.
Lubricate before you penetrate
Wait before you ejaculate
The marriage bed is not some one-off date.
Discover your partner, become intimate
Let her feel satisfied so she can reciprocate.

The reason she has another headache
Is because your slam-bams are beginning to irritate,
You roll over satisfied, but she lays awake
And she nudges you in the night
Because it is starting to frustrate
You are asleep but she is full of hate.

Take some time and keep in mind
That foreplay is subtle stimulation,
That playful expression that reminds you
The wife's breasts are also for the husband
Feast on those lips and look deep into her eyes
Before you realise, she'll be mesmerised
But for heaven's sake don't try to sell her your lies.

Death's Cold Touch

Her slim body laid stretched out on the couch
draped in her favour blue pyjamas
with the little yellow, red and white flowers.
She laid still as if asleep and every now and then
someone came to sneak a peek
at her pale cheek turning grey, and the tiny blue veins
forming lines, like vines running beneath her skin.
Her sister asked me to come in,
she sent the others away but said it was OK for me to stay.
She wanted me to pray because the ambulance was on its way.

As I reached to take the young girl's hand
the shocking coldness sent a shiver up my spine,
I almost flung her hand from mine
but caught myself, just in time.
I knelt beside the purple couch to pray
and pronounce my blessing.
Through the open window
I heard children playing in the street.
'Pass it to me,' a girl's voice called,
'I'm a girl but I can still kick a ball.'

Her sister came and closed the window,
she pulled the curtains tight,
within the little room, she captured the warmth
but blocked out the light.

The darkness in the room developed a mouldy smell,
or was it the girl on the couch, I could not tell.
Seventeen years old and her body laid still,
her life is slipping away,
her sister has so much confidence in me
and all I can do is pray.

They Said

My soul was in trouble
I didn't know what to do,
A friend took me to Church
And there I heard about You.

They said, You are the Saviour
A Friend of all mankind,
They said, my life would be so much better
If You were a Friend of mine.

They said, I could always reach You
At any time of day,
They said, You will always answer
When I fall on my knees in prayer.

They said, You will always listen
To everything I say,
They said, if I ever feel forsaken
You are the Truth, the Life, the Way.

They said, You are the Shepherd
And Bishop of my soul,
They said, You would keep me safe
Like a sheep within Your fold.

They said, You are the King
Who reigns in truth and love
They said, that You have a kingdom
Somewhere in heaven above.

They said, You died for me, Lord Jesus
That I might live for You,
They said, but I never paid attention
To what they said I must do.

And now I've left it all so very late
I've gambled and I've lost.
I never did accept You then
When they said You died upon the cross.

If only I could live my life again
Lord Jesus, I'll live it all for You,
And You would be my closest Friend
For now, I know, that all they said is true.

The Rapture

I woke up this morning and my wife was gone
I went to the bathroom for the light was on
But it was empty, it was empty
I rushed to the kitchen where I know she'll be
But she wasn't there, you see
I thought she was playing a trick on me
For today was our wedding anniversary.

I went to the kids' room, but they were not there
I thought they had gone jogging
Then I saw their gear,
And my son's iPhone on the floor beside his chair.
I had an uneasy feeling, I felt a pang of despair
I quickly switched on the radio,
A sad and sultry voice came on the air.

'Ladies and gentlemen, please do not fear
People are missing but we are still here,
We'll keep you informed as events unfold,
Hang on in there, be strong, be bold.'

It was a woman's voice, she sounded sincere
Then her voice choked up as she fought back a tear,
The world was in chaos as I thought it must be
I flicked to CNN on my cable TV
I listened to the stories of great catastrophes

Cars piled up, trains ran off their tracks, planes crashed
And mothers crying for their missing babies.

A big beardy man came on the air
His voice was husky but full of good cheer
As he tried to diagnose the problem for those
Whose hearts were now filled with fear,
'There is nothing much to all this mess
And it's not the end of the world as Christians suggest
It's just one of those things we can't explain
But here's some music to help ease your pain.'

The rock and roll music was loud and clear
And I wondered why CNN allowed that on the air
Then I realise they too were nearing despair.
One reporter was crying non-stop,
'Lord Jesus my husband is gone, and I am not!
No matter what they say I know what all this mean,
My husband was a Christian, but I was the dance-hall queen!
He tried to warn me, but I never listened,
Now he has gone to be with Jesus
And nothing they say is going to appease us.'

She fell on her knees with a heart-wrenching cry
I too started sobbing, I didn't want to die
I confessed my sin, opened my heart to let Jesus in
I was clinging to a straw, my chances were slim
Events were unfolding, my heart was beating fast
I remembered a sermon, that the harvest is past

I always thought salvation could wait,
Now I realised it was fatal mistake.

An alarm went off, I awoke in a sweat
My wife was still sleeping, she hadn't awakened yet
I shook her so hard she awoke with a stark
'What's the matter honey?' She cried out in the dark
I couldn't answer, the tears stuck in my throat
I fell to the floor as I started to choke,
She knelt beside me and put her hand on my head
It was as if she knew, she turned to me and said
'You can receive Jesus right here, right now, beside this bed.'

Friends this event is true,
One day millions will go missing
And one could be you,
Gone to place of eternal peace and happiness
Free from death, pain or any kind of sickness
All we need to do is call on Jesus' name
He promised to save us
And life will never be the same.

Afterword

The Valley of Baca (Ps 84:1-12)

Some people see life as a race we must run; a fight we must engage in; a walk we must take; or simply a life we must live to the best of our ability.

No matter how we view life, the Valley of Baca brings us to the midpoint of our journey and forces us to reach deep into our spirit and muster whatever resources we find there and press on to the other side of our challenge.

The psalms reflect our journey from great expectations, through the valley of despair to our moments of triumphs and ecstatic praise.

Psalms 84 is described as a Hebrew sandwich style poem that teaches one of the greatest lessons about resilience when all seems lost. Verses one to five express a deep yearning for a place of safety, recognition, acceptance and provision, which readers of the Bible associate with the house of God.

Verses six and seven explore the challenges that make us stop and review our commitment and our determination to achieve our goal, reach our destination and grasp the reality of our hopes and dreams. All that we find in this valley is evidence of the hardship experienced by those who went before us.

Verses eight to twelve highlight the great benefits of those who achieved their goals, reached their destination and came away with greater rewards than they had imagined. It is the rewards of those who share their testimonies that encourage us to press through our valley, push past our tears and discover what is on the other side.

The experiences we undergo in Baca are not easy. Many families split up and marriages break apart in Baca. Many people give up on their goals and settle for a miserable or mediocre existence which eventually impacts negatively on their mental health and wellbeing. Many succumb to depression and low mood and many die in the Valley of Baca.

This valley separates our desire to achieve from our determination to achieve; the yearning for an outcome from doing what it takes to achieve that outcome. In Church we call it moving from the superficial act of praise to engaging in true worship from the heart which propels us into crazy praise as we pass through our valleys.

Although Baca is a place of weeping and dryness it helps us to understand what Jesus meant when He said, "I came that you may have life and have it more abundantly" (John 10:19). We learn to enjoy life to the full. At times life's circumstances paralyse us with fears and tears, and we cannot move until we learn to commit fully to our cause.

I have learnt that The Valley of Baca is where we change gears, roll up our sleeves and get down to brass tacks. Baca was the hardest place in my spiritual, emotional and financial experience, but it was also the place of my greatest rewards. I learnt to live the beatitudes while in this valley.

In my Journey Through Baca, I learnt the difference between being poor in spirit and being poor spirited. I learnt to mourn and not to moan; to be meek without becoming weak; to hunger and thirst after righteousness and not merely attend a Church service. I got to engage with and draw strength from those who are sincere in their pursuit and to recognise those who came along for the ride. The valley of Baca is the breaking point. It is where you make up your mind and purpose in your heart to make it, no matter what challenges come your way.

I am determined that if I can swim, I will swim, or I will hold on to the broken fragments of my dreams and ambitions and I will not let go until I make it to the other side of this valley.

I hope you are determined to do the same.

Thank you for taking this journey with me, through this valley of tears we call Baca.